A HISTORICAL ALBUM OF

NEBRASKA

A HISTORICAL ALBUM OF

NEBRASKA

Charles A. Wills

THE MILLBROOK PRESS, Brookfield, Connecticut

Front and back cover: "Approaching Chimney Rock," a painting by William Henry Jackson. Courtesy of the National Park Service, Scotts Bluff National Monument.

Title page: Cattle ranch, western Nebraska. Courtesy of the Nebraska Department of Economic Development.

Library of Congress Cataloging-in-Publication Data

Wills, Charles.
    A historical album of Nebraska / Charles A. Wills.
        p. cm. — (Historical albums)
    Includes bibliographical references (p. 62) and index.
    Summary: A history of Nebraska, from its early exploration and settlement to the state today.
    ISBN 1-56294-509-2 (lib. bdg.) ISBN 1-56294-852-0 (pbk.)
       1. Nebraska—History—Juvenile literature. 2. Nebraska—Gazetteers—Juvenile literature. I. Title. II. Series.
F666.3.W59 1994
978.2—dc20

94-37398
CIP
AC

 Created in association with Media Projects Incorporated

C. Carter Smith, *Executive Editor*
Lelia Wardwell, *Managing Editor*
Charles A. Wills, *Principal Writer*
Bernard Schleifer, *Art Director*
Shelley Latham, *Production Editor*
Arlene Goldberg, *Cartographer*

Consultant: Thomas Creigh, Jr., member of the Nebraska State Historical Society Executive Board and the Nebraska Historic Preservation Board.

CONTENTS

Introduction

Evening and the flat land,
Rich and somber and always silent;
The miles of fresh-plowed soil,
Heavy and black, full of strength and harshness.

Willa Cather, Nebraska's greatest writer, wrote these lines of poetry as an introduction to her 1913 novel *O Pioneers!*, a classic story of life on the Nebraska plains. Much of Cather's description still rings true more than eighty years later. Lying in the midst of the Great Plains, Nebraska remains a land of farms and ranches; of winds rippling vast fields of wheat and corn; of cattle grazing under a blue western sky.

Much has changed in Nebraska since Cather's day. Modern Nebraska is also a state of high-tech industry and thriving cities. But Nebraska remains a place where the past and present are closely linked. Drive west from Omaha on Interstate 80, for example, and you'll travel along the route taken by settlers on the Oregon Trail more than 150 years ago. Those travelers, in turn, followed in the footsteps of the fur traders and trappers of the 1700s and early 1800s. And those adventurers were newcomers compared to the Native Americans who hunted buffalo through Nebraska's plains and river valleys for centuries before the first white people arrived in the region.

As you continue on your trip, you might see a low mound of green in the distance—the remains of a sod house that was home to a pioneer family a century ago. These pioneers—including Willa Cather's parents—braved loneliness, drought, and other dangers to turn Nebraska into a great agricultural state. It took a special kind of toughness to make a success of farming or ranching on the plains. Even today, when most of the state's people live in towns and cities, Nebraskans are renowned for their rugged and independent spirit—a legacy of the state's proud history.

LAND OF THE FLAT WATERS

Swiss artist Karl Bodmer painted Bellevue, one of the oldest non-Indian settlements in Nebraska, as it appeared in the 1830s. Bellevue began as a fur-trading post in 1823.

The region that would become Nebraska was claimed by both France and Spain in the 16th and 17th centuries. Acquired by the United States in the Louisiana Purchase of 1803, Nebraska was seen as a "desert" by American explorers. Fur traders and pioneers used the Platte River Valley as a highway to the West, but Nebraska had few permanent settlers until it became a territory in 1854. The passage of the Homestead Act in 1862 and the coming of the railroads in the 1860s helped spur the region's growth, and in 1867 Nebraska joined the Union as the thirty-seventh state.

The People of the Plains

In prehistoric times, the middle of the North American continent was a vast inland ocean. Over millions of years, a great mountain range—the Rockies—thrust upward from the bottom of this ocean, tilting and draining the lands to either side. Later, rivers of ice called glaciers moved down from the north. When the glaciers retreated, they made the land east of the Rocky Mountains a region of mostly flat land—the Great Plains—cut through by rivers.

In the part of the plains that now forms the state of Nebraska, two rivers—the North Platte and the South Platte—combine into one river, which then drains eastward into the great Missouri River. The Platte is wide but shallow; 19th-century travelers joked that it was "an inch deep and a mile wide." Native Americans of the Oto nation called their homeland Nebrathka—"the land of flat waters"—the source of the state's name.

Today, we think of the Great Plains as a mostly treeless region. When the first Native Americans arrived in the area about 12,000 years ago, however, the plains were heavily forested. These first Nebraskans, called Paleo-Indians by scholars, lived by hunting now-extinct animals like the woolly mammoth. Over the centuries, chang-

Indians called this rock formation, which rises 800 feet above the plains, Meapate—"the hill that is hard to go around." American explorers later named it Scotts Bluff, after a fur trader who died near the site in 1828.

ing climate conditions caused the forests to give way to grasslands, and the Paleo-Indian Culture died out.

About 2,000 years ago, another Native American group arrived in Nebraska. These people are known as the Woodland Culture because they probably migrated from the wooded lands east of the Mississippi River. The Woodland people were hunters, but they also grew crops of corn, beans, and squash. They lived in semi-permanent villages and developed pottery. Like the Paleo-Indians before them, however, the Woodland people eventually disappeared from the plains, perhaps because of a long drought in the 14th century AD.

Over the next few centuries, Native American groups migrated to Nebraska from other parts of North America. The Oto, Ponca, Omaha, and Missouri groups came to live along the Missouri River. These tribes lived in permanent villages and practiced farming, but twice a year each village would travel west to hunt the vast herds of buffalo, or bison, that swarmed over the plains.

Along the Platte and other rivers of central Nebraska lived the Pawnees. The largest Indian nation in the region, the Pawnees numbered pehaps 10,000 people by the 18th century. The Pawnee way of life was similar to that of their neighbors to the east: It was a mix of hunting and farming. Religion was an important part of daily life. Ceremonies accompanied most Pawnee activities, and each Pawnee village treasured its bundle of sacred objects.

Western Nebraska was home to the Sioux, or Dakotas, members of a great Native American culture that lived throughout the Great Plains. Unlike the Pawnees, the Sioux were nomadic (they had no permanent homes) and they scorned farming. Instead, they depended on the buffalo, whose meat, hide, and bones provided them with food, shelter, and tools. South of the Sioux country lived the Arapahoes and Cheyennes, also nomadic, buffalo-hunting peoples.

The horse played a major role in the culture of Nebraska's Native Americans, as it did for Indian groups all over the plains region. Brought to North America by Spanish explorers and settlers in the 16th century, horses spread from the Southwest to the Great Plains by the mid-1700s. The horse gave the Plains peoples great mobility and made hunting the buffalo easier and less dangerous. Thus, Europeans had a great impact on Nebraska's Native Americans even before the first white people set foot in the region.

The Newcomers

In 1540, a Spanish expedition led by Francisco Vasquez de Coronado marched north from Mexico and reached the Great Plains. More than 150 years later, another Spanish leader, Juan de Oñate, also explored the plains. Probably neither man reached present-day Nebraska, but the Spanish government claimed the entire plains region as Spanish territory.

The Spanish soon had competition. By the late 1600s, French explorers and traders were exploring Canada and pushing south into the Mississippi River Valley. In 1682, Robert Cavalier, Sieur de la Salle, traveled down the Mississippi and claimed a vast stretch of land as French territory. La Salle named this land Louisiana, after Louis XIV, king of France.

Twenty years later, a Frenchman named Etienne de Bourgmont left the French fort at Detroit in present-day Michigan and headed west. Probably the first European to reach Nebraska, he settled in a Native American village on the Platte River.

Word of Bourgmont's journey eventually reached the Spanish governor in Santa Fe, capital of Spanish New Mexico. Rumors that the French were building outposts along the Platte River spread throughout the region. In fact, Bourgmont was only a deserter from the French army, and the reports of French colonists on the

On the plains, as in other parts of North America, the European colonial powers sought to make allies of the Native Americans in their struggles for territory. This 18th-century cartoon depicts France and Spain competing for the loyalty of a Native American warrior.

Platte were false. Governor Valverde, however, was convinced that France was trespassing on Spanish territory.

In 1719, Valverde led soldiers north to the Platte. They found no Frenchmen and returned to Santa Fe, but again Valverde heard rumors of a French presence in Nebraska. In 1720, Valverde sent out another armed expedition, this one led by Captain Pedro de Villasur.

Villasur and about 100 troops— forty Spanish soldiers and sixty Indian warriors—reached the junction of the Platte and Loup rivers in the summer of 1720. While the soldiers slept on the morning of August 13, a Pawnee war party swept down on their camp. Villasur and all but thirteen soldiers

were killed; the survivors fled back to Santa Fe.

Villasur's defeat discouraged Spanish exploration of the Nebraska region. The next Europeans in the area were two French brothers, Pierre and Paul Mallet, who crossed Nebraska from east to west in 1739.

Spain and France continued to press their conflicting claims to the Louisiana Territory until 1763, when the Treaty of Paris ended the French and Indian War. The treaty granted the Louisiana Territory (including Nebraska) to Spain.

Captain Pedro de Villasur and 100 soldiers were attacked by a Pawnee war party while camped near the Platte and Loup rivers. This detail of a painting done on an animal hide by an unknown artist shows the battle in great detail.

The Great American Desert

It hardly mattered which nation "owned" Nebraska, at least as far as the land's inhabitants—the Native Americans—were concerned. Neither France nor Spain had founded any permanent settlements in the region. For the rest of the 18th century, the only white people to visit Nebraska were a few traders and trappers of various nationalities. They came in search of furs which would fetch a high price in the markets of Europe.

Still, even this minor contact was significant for the native peoples. The Pawnees, Omahas, and other tribes were glad to gain guns and tools from the traders, but not everything the whites brought was welcome. Many Indians fell victim to the rum and whisky that the traders also offered in return for furs.

Even more deadly were the unfamiliar diseases, like smallpox, that appeared along with the whites. Epidemics sometimes carried off

Vast herds of buffalo roamed Nebraska's plains when the first American explorers and settlers arrived in the region. One traveler wrote, "I could stand on my wagon & see more than 10,000 . . . the Plain was perfectly black with them on both sides of the [Platte] River . . . "

entire villages. By the beginning of the 19th century, Nebraska's Native American population was in decline.

Events in Europe set the stage for a new era in Nebraska. In 1800, French dictator Napoléon Bonaparte secretly forced Spain to return the Louisiana Territory to France. Napoléon imagined a new French empire in North America, but his scheme never got off the ground.

In 1803, President Thomas Jefferson sent a diplomatic mission to France. The purpose of the mission was to secure American trading rights in the port of New Orleans, but to the Americans' surprise, the French government offered to sell the entire Louisiana Territory. The diplomats agreed to pay France a bargain price of $15 million for the land, Jefferson persuaded Congress to approve the sale, and the size of the United States doubled practically overnight.

The huge territory, which extended from the Mississippi River to the Rocky Mountains, was largely unexplored. Jefferson quickly authorized an exploring expedition to be led by his secretary, Meriwether Lewis, and an army officer, William Clark. In the summer of 1804, the party of forty-five made its way up the Missouri River. On July 21, the explorers arrived at the Platte River in present-day Nebraska.

Two weeks later, Lewis and Clark met with members of the Omaha and Oto nations on a cliff overlooking the Missouri River—a place known ever since as Council Bluffs. Clark recorded the meeting in his journal: "Delivered a long speech to them expressive of our journey, [and] the wishes of our government." Lewis and Clark continued their journey believing the Indian leaders would happily obey American authority. Actually, the "leaders" the explorers met with had no real power; the true leaders of the local Native Americans were off on the summer buffalo hunt. It was only one of a long series of misunderstandings between whites and Native Americans in Nebraska and the rest of the West.

A small but steady stream of travelers passed through Nebraska in the next few years. In 1806, Lieutenant Zebulon Pike of the U.S. Army raised the American flag over the Republican River. Traders like Spanish-American Manuel Lisa continued to comb the region for buffalo furs and beaver pelts. In fact, the traders probably did more to open up Nebraska than official expeditions like Pike's. In the words of one Nebraska historian, "The map of the West was indeed first drawn on a beaver skin."

The valuable fur commerce soon attracted the attention of British traders, who began operating along the upper Missouri River. Fearing British competition and also British influence over the region's Native Americans, Congress decided to build military posts along the Missouri. In 1819,

This 1810 woodcut shows Lewis and Clark meeting with Omaha and Oto Indians at Council Bluffs in August, 1804. In his diary, Clark described the scenery around Council Bluffs: "The most beautiful prospect of the [Missouri] River up and Down the country presented it self which I ever beheld."

more than 1,000 troops went up the Missouri aboard five steamboats—the first such vessels ever seen this far west. Unfortunately, the steamboats ran aground a few miles below Council Bluffs. The soldiers abandoned the steamboats for flat-bottomed boats, brought their supplies upriver, and built a large fort, named after their commander, General Henry Atkinson, very close to the site of Lewis and Clark's meeting with the Otos and Omaha tribes.

The next year, another major expedition set out across Nebraska toward the Rocky Mountains led by Major Stephen Long. Major Long called the dry, mostly treeless plains "the Great American desert." The region, he reported, was ". . . almost wholly unfit for cultivation [farming], and

In the 1820s, the American Fur Company built four steamboats for use in the shallow waters of the upper Missouri River. This painting shows one of them, the *Yellowstone*, fighting the current upriver in 1837.

of course uninhabitable by a people depending on agriculture for their subsistence."

Long was wrong. The plains may have looked like a desert to people raised among the trees and hills of the eastern United States, but the soil was fertile. And despite the area's low rainfall, there was plenty of underground water—especially in what would become Nebraska—to irrigate crops. Still, the accounts of Long and other explorers convinced most Americans that settling the plains would be an impossible task.

In 1827, with the fur trade in decline, the army abandoned Fort Atkinson. Six years later, the land we now call Nebraska was declared an "Indian Territory," land that would be preserved for Indian settlement.

The Way West

Nebraska first became important to the United States as a passageway to the lands farther west. The reasons for this have to do with the region's geography. Nebraska's major rivers flow from west to east, rather than from north to south, so travelers moving west had few bodies of water to cross. Also, the Platte River Valley provided an excellent highway across the Great Plains to the passes of the Rocky Mountains.

Fur trappers and Christian missionaries traveling to and from the Pacific Coast had used the Platte route as early as 1813, but it wasn't until the early 1840s that the great westward migrations got under way. The destination of choice for many settlers was the fertile "Oregon Country" of the Pacific Northwest. From 1843 until the Civil War, more than 500,000 pioneers traveled the famous Oregon Trail, of which the Platte River Valley formed a major part.

Wagon guides—hardy, experienced frontier travelers—led the wagon trains that rolled through Nebraska on the way to Oregon or California. This engraving shows the scene at the end of the day's travel: guides relaxing by the campfire to the tune of a fiddle as pioneer families prepare for the night.

For pioneers, the journey west began in late spring at jumping-off points like Independence, Missouri. After building or buying canvas-topped wagons, the families would form a wagon train, often command-ed by an experienced guide. After crossing the Missouri on flatboat fer-ries, they traveled two or three weeks to reach Fort Kearny, an army post on the Platte, where the journey across the plains began in earnest.

Travel along the "Great Platte River Road," as the Oregon Trail was also known, meant both hardship and excitement for the Oregon-bound pioneers. Each day's journey began at sunrise and ended at sunset; if the travelers were lucky, their oxen-drawn wagons might cover fifteen to twenty miles during that time. But sudden summer storms, broken wagon axles, and runaway livestock could hold up a wagon train for hours or days.

The pioneers marveled at scenery like Chimney Rock and Scotts Bluff—rock formations that towered above the surrounding grassland. At night, with the wagons drawn into a circle and the livestock turned loose to graze, there might be card games, singing, or Bible readings.

Diaries of Oregon-bound pioneers are full of worries about attacks by Indians. In fact, attacks on wagon trains were rare, and when they did happen the attackers were usually more interested in running off cattle and horses for their own herds than in

A wagon train crosses the Platte River in this 19th-century painting by William Henry Jackson. A pioneer song describes the Platte Valley route to the West: "There's not a log to make a seat/along the River Platte/So when you eat you've got to stand/or sit down square and flat."

killing the emigrants. More likely, bands of Native Americans would simply demand a few head of cattle as a "toll" for crossing their lands.

The journey through Nebraska was the easy part of the trip. After leaving the river valleys behind, the travelers faced a steep and dangerous climb over the Rockies before they finally reached the green valleys of Oregon.

Oregon wasn't the only destination of the homesteaders passing through Nebraska in the 1840s and 1850s. Two other major trails—the Mormon Trail and the California Trail—also made use of the Platte River Valley, and carried pioneers to present-day Utah and California.

The Mormons—members of a religious group founded in western New York state in the 1820s—had been driven out of Illinois and Missouri by 1844. After the murder of the group's founder, Joseph Smith, Mormon leader Brigham Young decided the only way to escape persecution was to move far to the west.

In 1846, Young founded a Mormon community, Winter Quarters, not far from what is now the city of Omaha, Nebraska. In the spring, Young and 143 other pioneers left Winter Quarters and journeyed along the Platte, finally reaching Great Salt Lake in Utah. The following year, Young led 2,500 Mormons to the recently founded settlement of Salt Lake City along the Mormon Trail. (The Mormon Trail ran parallel to the Oregon Trail through Nebraska, but the Mormons generally kept to the north side of the Platte River, the Oregon-bound pioneers to the south.) Several thousand more Mormons followed the trail to Salt Lake City in the 1850s.

Another big group of travelers to pass through Nebraska was looking not for new land or religious freedom, but gold. In 1848, that precious metal was found in California, a territory just won from Mexico by the United States. By the summer of 1849 thousands of people were on their way to the gold fields by way of the Platte and the South Pass in the Rockies— the California Trail. Less organized than the Oregon pioneers or the Mormons and often unprepared for the hardships of life on the trail, many of these "forty-niners" died of disease and sometimes starvation. Still, probably more than 100,000 fortune-hunters made the overland journey to California before the "gold fever" began to fade in the 1850s.

Territorial Years

During the years of the westward migrations, present-day Nebraska was part of a "Permanent Indian Frontier" stretching from the Platte River to the Red River far to the south. Congress didn't organize this "Indian Territory" to preserve the traditional lands of the Pawnees, Sioux, and other Plains peoples; instead, the government used the land to resettle Native Americans who had been driven from their homelands east of the Mississippi River. In fact, Nebraska's Indians lost much of their land in the process; for example, an 1833 treaty forced the Pawnees to transfer their lands south of the Platte to the federal government.

Although white settlement was forbidden in this Indian Territory, a few settlers did arrive in the region during this time. They realized that Nebraska (the name came into common use around 1842) was hardly the barren desert described by Stephen Long. These "Nebraska Boomers" soon called on Congress to officially organize a Nebraska Territory.

It was the prospect of a transcontinental railroad, however, that sparked the first major movement for territorial status. Most Americans now agreed

The Horse Creek Treaty of 1851 set aside much of western Nebraska as a reservation for the Sioux nation. This map, drawn by the famous missionary Pierre Jean de Smet, shows the boundaries of the Sioux land.

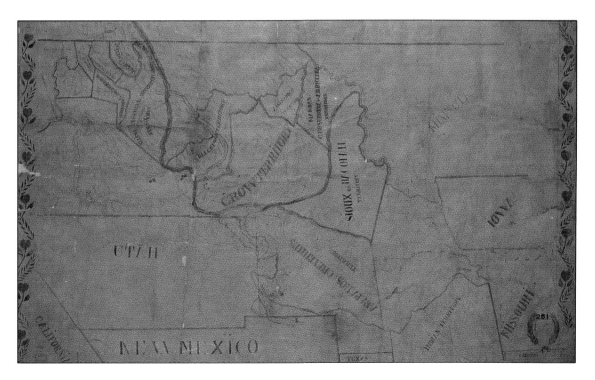

that a cross-country railroad had to be built to connect the West Coast with the East. The question was, which route should the proposed railroad take? To Stephen Douglas, a young Democratic representative from Illinois, a route through the Platte Valley seemed a natural choice.

The route favored by Douglas and his supporters would run right through the Permanent Indian Frontier. Congress would have to reorganize part of the region into a territory before construction could begin. In 1844, Douglas introduced a bill to do just that, but congressmen from the Southern states voted to defeat it.

The South's opposition had to do with the great political issue of the era—slavery. According to the Missouri Compromise of 1820, slavery was forbidden in land north of the 36th parallel of latitude—a region that included the proposed Nebraska Territory. Nebraska would thus be a free (non-slave) territory and eventually a free state. This would upset the delicate balance of power between the North and South in Congress.

Douglas continued to press for the railroad and the territory after he was elected to the Senate in 1848, but his efforts were in vain. In 1854, Douglas proposed a compromise in the form of the Kansas-Nebraska Act. Under its terms, two new territories—Kansas and Nebraska—would be organized. The Missouri Compromise would be set aside in favor of what Douglas called "popular sovereignty"—the people of the new territories would decide for themselves whether to allow slavery. This satisfied the South, and the bill passed.

On May 30, 1854, the Territory of Nebraska was officially organized. The territory was far larger than the present state; its boundaries extended to the Rockies and north to the Canadian border. Despite its vast size, the territory held only about 3,000 non-Native American residents, almost all of whom lived along the Missouri and Platte rivers.

President Franklin Pierce appointed Francis Burt as the territory's first governor, but Burt died just two days after reaching the territory. Thomas B. Cuming, his successor, decided to locate the capital at tiny Omaha City.

The decision caused hard feelings among the residents of Bellevue, Nebraska's oldest settlement, who felt their community was the logical site for the capital.

Settlement was slow: Over the next seven years, only about 27,000 settlers arrived in the territory.

By the 1850s, some pioneers began to see Nebraska as a place to settle instead of just a route to the lands farther west. This 1850 photograph (opposite), one of the earliest depictions of settler life in Nebraska, shows a pioneer cabin on the banks of the Niobrara River.

The Republican party was established after the passage of the Kansas-Nebraska Act of 1854. This political cartoon (below) shows John C. Frémont, the party's first presidential candidate. He is riding an old, weak horse, the cartoonist's symbol for the antislavery issue.

The Road to Statehood

There were a few slaves in the Nebraska Territory, but most of its citizens were opposed to slavery. In fact, some Nebraskans operated a western division of the Underground Railroad, a system for smuggling escaped slaves to freedom in the Northern states or across the border to Canada.

In April 1861, the tensions between North and South over slavery finally exploded into civil war. Nebraska was far from the fighting, but more than 3,000 citizens left the territory to fight in the Union Army—a remarkable number considering the small size of the territorial population.

While the Civil War raged, Congress passed two bills that greatly influenced Nebraska's history. The first was the Homestead Act of 1862. The act granted 160 acres of public (government-owned) land to any settler willing to settle on and improve it for at least five years. The first homestead in Nebraska went to Daniel Freeman, a soldier in the Union Army. Freeman had to report to an army post on January 1, 1863, the day the Homestead Act went into effect, so, according to legend, he talked a local official into opening his office just after midnight so he could file his claim.

The second law was the Pacific Railroad Act, also passed in 1862, which finally authorized construction of a transcontinental railroad by way of the Platte Valley. The Union Pacific company began laying track westward from Omaha in 1865. By 1867, the rails passed what is now the western border of the state. Two years later the Union Pacific linked up with the Central Pacific, which laid track eastward from California.

The steel rails were Nebraska's lifeline. Practically all Nebraska towns west of Omaha were founded on or near the railroad, which gave farmers a way to ship their crops to market. The Union Pacific and the railroads that followed made it easy for new settlers to reach the territory—an important consideration, because the territory's rivers were too shallow for most steamboats.

During and after the Civil War, Congress created new states and territories out of the vast Nebraska Territory, until its borders resembled those

This 1861 photograph (top) shows Nebraska volunteers aboard a steamboat on their way to join the Union Army. They are probably members of the 1st Nebraska Regiment, organized in June 1861, just two months after the Civil War began.

This photograph was taken in October 1866, when the Union Pacific's track reached the 100th meridian of longitude, roughly the halfway point of its route through Nebraska.

of the present state. By the end of the war, the territory's population passed the 50,000 mark, and in 1866, the territorial legislature adopted a state constitution. The Nebraska Territory was on its way to becoming a state.

Just as the slavery controversy held up the creation of a Nebraska Territory, however, political issues delayed statehood. Although most Nebraskans had opposed slavery, many of the territory's citizens wanted to discourage newly freed slaves from settling in Nebraska. Thus, the 1866 constitution forbade blacks from voting. Congress refused to consider Nebraska for statehood until the restriction was removed.

The territorial legislature agreed to revise the constitution, and Congress passed a statehood bill toward the end of 1866. On March 1, 1867, Nebraska officially joined the Union as the thirty-seventh state.

In an action that angered many Omahans, the state legislature voted to establish Nebraska's capital at Lancaster, a tiny settlement far out on the plains. The new capital was renamed Lincoln in honor of the murdered president, and on December 1, 1868, the state government moved into a new capitol building.

After Emancipation (freedom), many freed slaves headed west to start a new life. In this 1865 photograph, African Americans pose for a picture in downtown Brownsville, Nebraska.

PART TWO

THE CORNHUSKER STATE

The State Fair was an event Nebraska's rural families looked forward to each year. This Currier & Ives lithograph shows officials judging livestock in a competition at a typical state fair.

In the 1870s and 1880s, farmers and cattle ranchers turned Nebraska into an agricultural state. An economic boom at the beginning of the 20th century stalled when crop prices fell in the 1920s, and the state experienced great hardship during the Depression of the 1930s. During and after World War II, Nebraska's farms prospered again thanks to advances in irrigation and mechanization. The state's economy became more diverse. After the 1960s, Nebraska experienced a population shift, with more and more of the state's people living in towns and cities—but farming and ranching continue to make Nebraska one of the nation's greatest agricultural states.

War on the Plains

"A great flood is coming, will soon be here. I am old and near the grave. I may be gone before it comes but I am sure it will come. The wild animals which God has given us for sustenance will disappear, even the birds will have no resting place; some of you may not understand my meaning but if you do, prepare yourselves . . . ."

So said Big Elk, a chief of the Omaha nation, when the first white settlers and travelers reached Nebraska. In the 1860s and 1870s, the flood of white settlement Big Elk spoke of washed over Nebraska and the rest of the plains. Thousands of farmers, ranchers, hunters, and railroad workers invaded Indian homelands, pushing settled tribes such as the Omahas onto small reservations and destroying the buffalo herds on which nomadic peoples like the Sioux and Cheyennes depended. But in many places, including Nebraska, Native Americans tried to resist the pressure of white settlement. Years of bloodshed and terror followed, for settlers and Native Americans alike.

The first major clashes in Nebraska came in the territorial years. In 1855, an argument between a Sioux band and some Mormon travelers led to the brutal destruction of a Sioux village by the U.S. Army. Then, in 1864, railroad and telegraph construction crews reached western Nebraska. In August of that year, the Sioux and their allies, the Arapahoes and Cheyennes, swept through the Platte Valley, burning isolated farms and ranches and killing many settlers. Again, the army moved in to protect the settlers, but clashes continued into the late 1860s.

While Native Americans tried to hold back white settlement, they also fought among themselves as they had for centuries. In fact, one of the greatest battles fought in Nebraska was not between settlers and Indians, but between the Sioux and Pawnees. In 1873, a Sioux band attacked 700 Pawnees camped along the Republican River near the present-day town of Trenton. Troops arrived to protect the Pawnees, but not before many had been killed. The survivors gave

In the years following the Civil War, the near-extinction of the buffalo rivaled white settlement and warfare in the destruction of the Native Americans' way of life. Hunters, like the ones shown here (opposite, top), killed hundreds of thousands of buffalo for their fur, or simply for sport, until only a handful remained.

Native Americans and construction crews sometimes clashed during the railroad-building years of the 1860s and 1870s. In this 1869 engraving (right) from *Harper's Weekly* newspaper, Native Americans attack a Union Pacific handcar near the Platte River.

29

up on Nebraska and agreed to move to a reservation in what is now the state of Oklahoma.

The federal government forced or persuaded other Nebraskan peoples to give up their lands and move to Indian Territory. One such group were the Poncas. In 1877, soldiers forced the tribe to migrate to the territory. Within two years, however, between one third and one half of the Poncas were dead from disease or hunger. Standing Bear, the Ponca chief, and a few of his people decided to return to their land in Nebraska. They made it home only to be captured by soldiers and imprisoned.

Standing Bear, aided by sympathetic whites, took the Poncas' case to court. In a rare legal victory for Native Americans, a federal judge ruled that "an Indian is a person within the meaning of the law." Standing Bear was freed, and a year later those Poncas who wanted to return to Nebraska from Indian Territory were allowed to do so.

By this time the conflict on the Great Plains was reaching its climax. When northern Sioux and Cheyennes overwhelmed Lt. Colonel George Custer's 7th Cavalry at the Battle of Little Bighorn (in present-day Montana) in July 1876, the U.S. Army launched a massive campaign to break the resistance of the Plains peoples once and for all. Many Cheyennes and Sioux were captured and imprisoned at Fort Robinson in Nebraska. Among them was the great Sioux war chief Crazy Horse, who was killed by soldiers in a scuffle on September 7, 1877.

Some northern Cheyennes were shipped south to Indian Territory. In the winter of 1878, a small band of Cheyennes led by Dull Knife escaped from the territory and made a desperate march across the frozen plains of Kansas and Nebraska, but were captured again. "We are home," said Dull Knife when told his people would be sent back to Indian Territory, "You may kill us but you can never make us leave our lands again." In January 1878, Dull Knife's Cheyennes made another bid for freedom by escaping from Fort Robinson. Many were killed in the escape, and the remainder were killed or captured over the next few weeks.

The epic of the Cheyennes marked the end of the long struggle between Native Americans and whites in Nebraska. Over the next decade, the army herded the last free bands of Plains peoples onto reservations or into Indian Territory. The year 1890 saw the last armed clash between whites and Indians. It ended with the massacre of several hundred Sioux by U.S. troops along a creek called Wounded Knee, just a few miles north of the Nebraska border in the Dakota Territory.

A Pawnee family poses outside its earth house near Loup, Nebraska, in this 1871 photograph (opposite). In 1875, after years of conflict with the Sioux and other Native American nations, Nebraska's once-powerful Pawnees were moved to a reservation in Indian Territory (the present-day state of Oklahoma), far to the south of their traditional homeland.

The northern Cheyenne war leaders Dull Knife (sitting) and Little Wolf refused to accept resettlement to Indian Territory. Dull Knife eventually surrendered at Fort Robinson, where his people were locked up with no heat, food, or water. Many were killed when they attempted to escape the fort on January 9, 1877.

Years of Boom and Bust

Statehood, the Homestead Act, the coming of the railroads, and the opening of Native American land to white settlement all combined to begin a new chapter in Nebraska's history. In the years after the Civil War, scores of towns sprang up on the plains, enterprising farmers made the "Great American Desert" bloom with crops, and ranchers brought countless head of cattle to graze on the state's western grasslands. From 1867 to 1874, the state's population went from about 50,000 residents to almost 250,000. By 1890, nearly a million people called Nebraska home.

Land was what drew most settlers to Nebraska. Many pioneer families obtained farms under the Homestead Act. Others bought their land from the railroads. The federal government granted huge tracts of public land to the Union Pacific and other railroads. The railroads, in turn, offered land for sale to newcomers. To encourage land

Native Americans, hunters, and immigrants mingle on the platform of Omaha's Union Pacific railroad depot in this engraving from the early 1880s. An average of 100,000 people per year settled in Nebraska between 1880 and 1890.

African Americans—including former slaves, like the family shown here—joined the flood of settlers arriving in Nebraska in the decades following the Civil War.

sales, the railroads cut their passenger rates and advertised the joys of Nebraska in newspapers and pamphlets. Railroad agents even traveled to Europe to persuade people to move to the state.

Many heeded the call. Immigrants from Europe arrived in Nebraska by the thousands in the 1870s and 1880s—English and Irish, Russians, Scandinavians, Czechs, and especially Germans. Still, three-quarters of the people who came to Nebraska after the Civil War were American-born. These settlers included Union Army veterans trying their luck in the West and African Americans—both freed slaves and escaped slaves who had fled to Canada on the Underground Railroad and returned after the Civil War ended slavery.

Wherever they came from, Nebraska pioneers endured a harsh existence. On the treeless plains, families built their homes from sod—blocks of soil—earning the pioneers the nickname sodbusters. Farms were far apart, and many families led a lonely, isolated existence. Raising a crop of wheat or corn meant long days of backbreaking work for all but the youngest family members.

All too often, natural disasters ruined months of hard work in a matter of hours. Wildfires and tornadoes frequently swept across the plains,

devastating everything in their path. In 1874 and 1875, swarms of grasshoppers plagued the state, turning the daytime sky dark as night when they descended to destroy fields of crops.

Some pioneers moved back east. A traveler reported finding a sign nailed to the door of an abandoned sod house that said: "This claim for sale. Four miles to the nearest neighbor. Seven miles to the nearest schoolhouse. Fourteen miles to the nearest town. Two hundred feet down to the nearest water. God bless our home!" But most stayed, hoping to prosper by hard work and determination.

In western Nebraska, where low rainfall made farming even tougher, people began raising cattle in the 1880s. Herds of Texas longhorns were driven north to graze on the Nebraska grasslands, and investors from New York to London raised money to set up huge ranches. Unfortunately, overgrazing and a series of unusually harsh winters in the mid-1880s killed thousands of

Homesteaders in central Nebraska's Custer County pose for a photograph (opposite, top). Houses like this one were made from foot-long blocks of sod, stacked like bricks, with a sod roof atop log poles. Note the cow grazing on the roof.

While flames from a prairie fire spread along the horizon, a Nebraska farmer quickly plows across his field in this illustration (left). By clearing a wide strip of land, called a fireguard, the farmer hopes to halt the wall of flames before it reaches his crops.

cattle and drove many ranchers out of business. Cattle farming in Nebraska didn't recover from these disasters until the early 1900s.

Nebraskans established an enduring custom during the boom-and-bust years of the 1870s and 1880s. Julius Sterling Morton, who came to Nebraska just before it became a territory, was one of the state's most prominent citizens. Morton believed that Nebraskans needed to plant trees in order to provide shade, fruit, timber, and fuel for future generations. He planted thousands of trees on his own land and persuaded his neighbors to do the same. In 1872, Morton convinced the state legislature to set aside April 10 as "Arbor Day"—a day for people to plant trees throughout the state.

By the end of the day on April 10, more than one million seedlings had been planted in Nebraska's soil. Arbor Day was so successful that it was repeated in following years, and the idea was adopted by other states as well. In 1885, the Nebraska legislature changed the date of Arbor Day to April 22—Morton's birthday—and made it a legal holiday.

Nebraska's major towns also grew during this time. Omaha enjoyed a boom in the 1880s thanks to the building of stockyards and meat-packing plants. By 1890, Omaha's population surpassed 125,000. Lincoln, Nebraska's capital and the site of the fine new state university, grew almost as fast as its long-standing rival.

The Populist Decade

Nebraska's farmers enjoyed good harvests for much of the 1880s. At the end of the decade, however, a period of drought set in, destroying crops and making life miserable for the farmers and small-town merchants and business people who depended on them. By 1891, about 20,000 Nebraskans, no longer able to make a living on the land, left the state.

Many farmers were angry at the railroads, which seemed to take unfair advantage of their rural customers. Railroads kept freight rates high, even in hard times, and owned by different companies, railroads combined to "fix" rates instead of competing for the farmer's dollar.

In response, a new political movement called populism sprang up in the agricultural West. The Populists called for government to regulate the railroads and take other actions to benefit hard-pressed farmers. Populism proved especially strong in Nebraska. When the national Populist organization, the People's Party, met to choose a presidential candidate for the election of 1892, the party chose Omaha as the site for its convention.

The People's Party candidate, James Baird Weaver, received more than a million votes, and Nebraska sent the first Populist senator to

Washington in the same year. For the rest of the decade, the Populists, allied with the Democrats, controlled Nebraska's state government. The Populists oversaw many reforms, including laws against child labor and regulation of the railroads and public utilities.

The Populists also wanted to change the national financial system. At this time, U.S. currency was based on the value of gold. The Populists wanted to increase the use of silver; they believed this plan would increase the amount of money in circulation, thus making it easier for farmers to pay off their debts. Bankers and industrialists in the East, however, felt that changing the system would weaken the U.S.

This photograph (opposite) shows a prosperous cattle ranch in Custer County as it appeared in the mid-1880s. By the end of the decade, blizzards and overgrazing had ruined much of Nebraska's ranches, while drought and poor harvests spelled disaster for the state's farmers.

This bank in Sargent (below) was one of many Nebraska businesses to fail in the hard times of the early 1890s. Nebraska's Populists believed easier credit and more coinage of silver would revive the state's hard-hit economy.

economy, which was floundering for much of the 1890s.

The loudest voice calling "free silver" belonged to Nebraska's own William Jennings Bryan, an Illinois-born lawyer and newspaper editor who had come to the state in 1887. In the early 1890s, his passionate speeches in support of populist reforms won him national attention. When the election year of 1896 arrived, Bryan captured both the Democratic and People's Party nominations for president. Bryan delivered a stunning pro-silver speech at the Democratic Convention, but he was defeated by Republican William McKinley in the election.

By the turn of the century, populism was in decline nationwide, although Populists remained powerful in Nebraska politics for many years.

American politician James Baird Weaver (top) was nominated as the Populist party's candiate for the 1892 presidential election at the party convention in Omaha. Although he lost the election, Weaver received more than a million popular votes.

Often called "the Great Commoner," William Jennings Bryan sought the presidency three times without success. This poster (right) is from the election of 1900, in which he was again defeated by Republican William McKinley. Bryan also served as secretary of state from 1913 to 1915.

Culture and Agriculture

Nebraska entered the 20th century with a population of slightly more than a million. About 150,000 were immigrants; of Nebraskans born in the United States, fully half were the children of immigrants. Most immigrants to the state continued to come from Northern Europe, but new ethnic groups began to arrive. Polish, Greek, and Italian laborers found work in the factories and meat-packing plants of Omaha. Japanese and Mexican farm hands could be found in many rural areas.

Agriculture in Nebraska revived in the early 1900s. The drought of the 1890s made the state's farmers painfully aware that they couldn't always depend on rainfall to water their crops. They needed an irrigation system to bring water from rivers and lakes to their fields. The first irrigation projects were built by private companies in the North Platte and Platte river valleys at the turn of the century. These systems used a series of canals and small dams to distribute the water

By 1900, when this photograph was taken, Nebraska's agricultural economy was reviving, and frame houses began to replace the log cabins and sod houses of the pioneers.

where it was needed. Previously dry, undeveloped land in these areas was now able to start producing crops on a large scale, thanks to irrigation.

Nebraska also worked to develop the Sand Hills, a region of rolling grass-covered hills with sandy soil in the northwestern corner of the state. In 1904, Congress passed the Kincaid Act. Sponsored by Nebraska representative Moses Kincaid, the act was an updated version of the Homestead Act. It offered 640 acres of Sand Hills land to anyone willing to farm in the region.

Once again, homesteaders headed west to break new ground under their plows. The Sand Hills, however, couldn't support most crops. Many "Kincaiders" sold their claims to ranchers, and once again western Nebraska became home to great herds of cattle. Unlike the ranchers of the 1880s, the cattle ranchers of the early 1900s took care to fence in their lands to prevent overgrazing. As a result, ranching flourished, and the western part of the state has been cattle country ever since.

While farmers and ranchers made Nebraska an agricultural powerhouse, Nebraska writers put the state on the nation's cultural map. One of the most important literary figures to come out of Nebraska was Willa Cather, who moved to the state from Virginia in 1883 at the age of ten. In novels like *O Pioneers!* (1913) and *My Antonia* (1918), Cather portrayed the harsh beauty of the Nebraska land-

scape and the tough, determined pioneers who made it their home.

Other notable Nebraska writers who have given wonderful accounts of the settlement of the state include Mari Sandoz and John G. Neihardt. Sandoz, a native of Sheridan County in the Sand Hills, made pioneer and Native American life her subject. Her first major work was *Old Jules*, a biography of her Swiss-born pioneer father. Sandoz later won fame for *The Cattlemen*, an account of the rise of ranching in western Nebraska.

John G. Neihardt's epic poem *A Cycle of the West* earned him official recognition as poet laureate of Nebraska in 1921. Also a student of Native American cultures (he lived with the Omaha nation for several years), Neihardt is best known today for *Black Elk Speaks* (1932), a biography of a Sioux spiritual leader.

After the United States entered World War I in 1917, almost 50,000 Nebraskans entered military service, and about 1,000 were killed. Nebraskans considered General John J. Pershing, commander of American forces in Europe, as one of their own. Although born in Missouri, Pershing spent part of his early army career at the University of Nebraska, as both teacher and student.

Agriculture flourished, as the state exported food not only to the rest of the country, but to the war-ravaged nations of Europe. A less positive wartime development was the perse-

The early 1900s also saw the revival of ranching in western Nebraska. Besides fencing in their lands to prevent overgrazing, ranchers improved cattle breeding and feed-raising techniques, which helped them to prosper. The rancher in this photograph (opposite) poses with some of his cattle.

Willa Cather reads to her younger brother and sister in this photograph (above) taken in the front yard of the family home in Red Cloud around 1900. Today the small house is part of the Willa Cather Historical Center.

cution of some Nebraskans of German birth or ancestry who were thought to be disloyal to the war effort. During the war years, several German-American pastors, teachers, and ordinary citizens were attacked and even jailed by so-called patriotic citizen's groups and courts.

In 1919, after the war ended, prejudice of a different kind hit Nebraska. When an African-American man was accused of attacking a white woman, a race riot broke out in Omaha. A mob of 5,000 people broke into the city courthouse and hung the accused man from a telephone pole. When the mayor stepped in to stop the violence, the mob tried to hang him, too.

In the early 1920s, Nebraska embarked on a major construction project: the building of a new state capitol building at Lincoln. Begun in 1922 and completed a decade later, the building with its 400-foot-high domed tower was hailed as a great architectural achievement.

To Nebraskans, the rise of the magnificent new building showed how far the state had come. Only a few decades before, the first pioneers had built their homes out of sod. Now a great limestone building towered over the plains.

Hard Times

The 1920s were prosperous years for much of America. For mostly agricultural states like Nebraska, however, the decade brought hard times. In the booming World War I years, many farmers had taken out mortgages to buy more land and bank loans to purchase tractors and other machinery.

Not long after the war ended, demand for farm products fell, and so did crop prices. A bushel of wheat that sold for $1.56 in 1920, for example, brought the farmer only 69 cents per bushel just four years later. Much of Nebraska's farm population found it impossible to pay off their debts; as a result, a quarter of the state's farms and more than 600 rural banks went out of business by the end of the decade.

The nationwide economic depression that set in after the Wall Street Crash of 1929 only made matters worse. So did a series of natural disasters. Nebraska went through a long period of drought in the 1930s; summer after summer of searing heat and low rainfall caused topsoil to blow

This photograph shows a common sight in the Nebraska of the 1920s and 1930s: An auctioneer sells the contents of a farm, which has been seized for debts. Some farmers greeted the auctioneer with a pitchfork—or a shotgun.

away in high winds, creating "dust bowl" conditions. When there wasn't too little water, there was too much. In 1935 the Republican River flooded, killing about 200 people and ruining many farms.

Debts, drought, and dust drove many people off the land and out of Nebraska. More than 60,000 people left the state in the 1930s. Those farmers who remained tried desperately to hold onto their land. Sometimes, farmers used force to resist sheriffs who had arrived to take possession of foreclosed property (farms whose owners couldn't pay their mortgages).

The state and federal governments stepped in to bring some relief to the state's citizens. In 1933, Governor

Charles Bryan introduced the first of several mortgage moratoriums forbidding seizure of foreclosed farms. This act gave banks and farmers the chance to work out repayment schemes at lower interest rates.

The federal Works Projects Administration (WPA) provided jobs to

Besides struggling farmers and unemployed workers, the WPA also helped out-of-work artists and writers during the Depression years. This farm scene (below) by Marguerite Zorach is one of many paintings, murals, and photographs produced by Nebraska artists working for the WPA.

To guard against soil loss, Nebraska farmers began surrounding their fields with shelter belts of trees in the 1930s as shown in this photograph (opposite). By breaking the force of the wind, the trees cut down on erosion.

farmers and townspeople who couldn't make ends meet on their own. Agencies like the Agricultural Adjustment Administration (AAA) sought to help farmers through government purchases of wheat, corn, and livestock. Other programs paid farmers to limit the amount of land they kept under cultivation.

Science helped, too. Agricultural engineers at the University of Nebraska explored new ways of halting erosion (loss of soil to wind and water). Farmers, remembering the advice of Julius Morton, planted more trees, this time as "shelter belts" to protect fields from winds.

In the midst of the terrible 1930s, Nebraska's government underwent a dramatic change. For two decades, Nebraska politicians had debated the merits of a unicameral (one-house) state legislature. Every state in the Union had a bicameral (two-house) legislature, but some Nebraskans questioned the wisdom of the traditional system.

Among these people was George W. Norris, the greatest politician to come out of Nebraska since William Jennings Bryan. Norris came to Nebraska in 1855 to practice law. His career in Washington began in 1902, when he was elected to the House of Representatives. In 1912 he won election to the Senate, where he remained until 1943. Norris was a Republican, but more often than not he went his own way instead of following the party line.

The fiercely independent senator had some strong ideas about govern-

Nebraska's chief justice swears in members of the state's first unicameral legislature in this photograph. The new system had a very practical benefit: Because a one-house legislature meant fewer lawmakers, the state government saved money—a fact that appealed to Nebraska voters in the lean times of the 1930s.

ment on the state level. Bicameral legislatures, argued Norris and his supporters, were simply a holdover from the English system of government. A legislature with one house, Norris believed, would be more democratic and better serve the needs of the state's people. Norris also called for state legislators to be elected on a nonpartisan basis—that is, lawmakers would answer to the people of their districts, not to the leaders of political parties.

In 1934, Nebraskans approved the change to a one-house, nonpartisan legislature in a statewide vote. In January 1937, the first reorganized legislature met in Lincoln. So far,

Nebraska is the only state to adopt a unicameral legislature.

The farm crisis eased a little in the late 1930s, when rainfall returned to normal, but Nebraska's farms and ranches still produced less in 1939 than a decade earlier. The state's factories and businesses, also hard hit by the Depression, were still in a slump as the decade drew to a close.

Recovery and Revival

In 1939, oil was discovered near Falls City in the southeastern part of the state. Thereafter, all development of oil and natural gas production occurred in western Nebraska. Although small compared to that of other western states like Texas and Oklahoma, Nebraska's new petroleum industry helped the state's economy climb out of the slump that resulted from the Great Depression.

The event that did the most to put Nebraska on the road to recovery was America's entry into World War II in December 1941. Once again, the products of Nebraska's farms and ranches were in great demand. Helped by years of above-average rainfall, farmers produced record crops of corn and wheat; by the time the war ended, more than 4 million head of beef cattle grazed the ranges of western Nebraska.

Grain and beef weren't Nebraska's only contributions to the war effort.

Corn tumbles into a storage pen at harvest time in this photograph. Although corn—and to a lesser extent, wheat—had been Nebraska's chief farm product since the sodbuster days, sorghum, alfalfa, soybeans, and other crops became increasingly important in the decades following World War II.

More than 120,000 Nebraskans served in the armed forces during the conflict, about 4,000 of whom lost their lives. Factories in Hastings, Grand Island, and other communities produced weapons and ammunition, while a major aircraft plant in Omaha turned out bombers for the U.S. Army Air Force. Old Fort Robinson, the post that had seen so much tragedy during the Indian Wars, became the center for the army's K-9 Corps, which trained dogs for wartime duties. Because of its flat terrain and clear skies, Nebraska was an ideal site for air bases. The U.S. Army Air Force built twelve major airfields in the state during World War II.

Nebraska's importance to the nation's defense continued after the war's end in August 1945. The relationship between the United States and the Soviet Union became one of mistrust and conflict. American military planners saw the need for a special force that could attack the Soviet Union with nuclear weapons if war ever broke out.

In 1946, the U.S. Army Air Force established the Strategic Air Command (SAC), a force of long-range nuclear bombers. Offutt Field, just south of Omaha, was chosen as SAC's headquarters. Offutt Air Force Base remained a key link in America's defensive chain for decades.

Nebraska's agriculture thrived in the years following World War II. The soil-conservation methods pioneered

A woman worker inspects bomb casings at an Omaha defense plant in 1944 in this photograph. Wartime factory orders boosted Nebraska's industry during World War II, while the renewed demand for grain and beef helped the state's agriculture climb out of the Depression.

in the Depression years were expanded throughout the state.

Irrigation also expanded during the war years. Nebraska's government had been funding large-scale irrigation projects since the 1920s, damming rivers and creating huge watering systems. Another important water source was the Ogallala aquifer, a vast underground reservoir located beneath central and southwestern Nebraska. To meet wartime food demands, farm owners drilled wells into the aquifer to irrigate those parts of their land that lay beyond existing water systems.

Increased use of tractors and other farm machinery helped make Nebraska's farms even more productive. In the 1950s, for example, the center-

Massive irrigation projects and the introduction of the center-pivot sprinkler led to record crop yields in the 1950s and 1960s. Farm machinery is expensive, however, and many Nebraska farmers went into debt trying to keep up with the new technology.

pivot sprinkler replaced older ditch-irrigation methods on many farms. By raising water pipes above fields, the new sprinkler irrigated crops evenly and efficiently.

Together, these innovations raised Nebraska's agricultural productivity to new heights. By 1963, the average Nebraska farm yielded almost fifty-four bushels of wheat per acre; forty years earlier, the yield was only about fifteen bushels per acre.

Nebraska Today

Nebraska's urban areas also grew in the post-World War II era. In the years between 1945 and 1960, Omaha's population increased by a third, while Lincoln's leapt by more than 50 percent. In 1940, Nebraska had only six communities with populations of more than 10,000. By 1990, that number had risen to fifteen. Today, about six out of every ten Nebraskans live in urban areas.

The movement from farm to town was made possible by mechanized agriculture, which greatly reduced the amount of labor needed to raise crops. With machines taking the place of people on the state's farms, more and more Nebraskans found work in towns and cities. As a result, industries like insurance, banking, and manufacturing joined farming and ranching as mainstays of the state's economy in the decades following World War II. In the 1980s and 1990s, high-tech companies came to the state.

Still, agriculture remains the engine that drives Nebraska's economy. Many businesses—Omaha's food-processing plants, for example—rely on the prod-

The skyline of Omaha, Nebraska's biggest city, stands in contrast to the plains that roll away toward the west. Omaha's importance as a transportation hub and a center for food-processing, manufacturing, data-processing, and insurance has made it one of the most vital cities in the West.

ucts of the state's farms and ranches. A dip in crop prices or a fall in demand for beef cattle can result in unemployment in Nebraska's cities. For these reasons, Nebraska's government and people pay close attention to the state's farms and ranches.

By the early 1970s, many Nebraskans worried that the state's agriculture might become a victim of its own success. Irrigation made farms more productive and eased traditional fears of drought, but irrigation also created problems. Most of the state's irrigation water comes from underground sources, so there are frequent arguments about ownership of water. There is also concern that water is being taken out of Nebraska's underground reserves faster than it can be replaced. Nebraskans also worry about the long term effect of chemical fertilizers and insecticides on the state's environment.

An agricultural problem of a different kind led the state government to propose a controversial law in 1982. For many years, Nebraska's farms had grown in size. Many small farmers couldn't afford the expensive machinery that had become a major part of farming on the plains. As a result, large-scale, corporation-run farms replaced small family farms throughout the state. In a statewide vote, Nebraskans approved the Family Farm Preservation Act. The new law limited the sale of family-owned farms to agricultural corporations.

Although not as badly hit as other states, Nebraska suffered during the nationwide farm crisis of the mid-1980s, when falling land values drove many farmers into bankruptcy. Today, however, Nebraska's economy is generally sound, thanks in large part to the state government's careful financial management.

Nebraska politicians have made an impact on the national scene in recent years. Omaha-born Gerald Ford became the first Nebraska native in the White House when he became president following Richard Nixon's resignation in 1974. In 1986, Nebraska made history as the first state to hold a governor's race in which both major-party candidates were women. Republican Kay Orr defeated Democrat Helen Boosalis.

Today, the most prominent Nebraskan in politics is Lincoln-born Democrat Bob Kerrey, a former governor (1982–86) who was elected to the Senate in 1988. Kerrey was a serious contender for the Democratic nomination in the presidential election of 1992.

Nebraska in the 1990s faces many challenges—first and foremost, perhaps, is the need to preserve the richness of the land on which so many people depend. From the days of the sodbusters, however, Nebraskans have always faced the future with a mix of innovation and determination. They will certainly continue to do so as the 21st century approaches.

Memorial Stadium in Lincoln (right) is always filled when the University of Nebraska Cornhuskers football team plays a home game. Nebraskans are so devoted to the team that the state legislature officially changed Nebraska's nickname from the Treeplanter's State to the Cornhusker State in 1945.

Lincoln-born and educated at the University of Nebraska, Robert Kerrey lost a leg and won the Congressional Medal of Honor in Vietnam. After starting a restaurant chain, Kerrey entered politics in 1981 with a successful run for governor. He is shown in this photograph (below) during a visit at a Nebraska school.

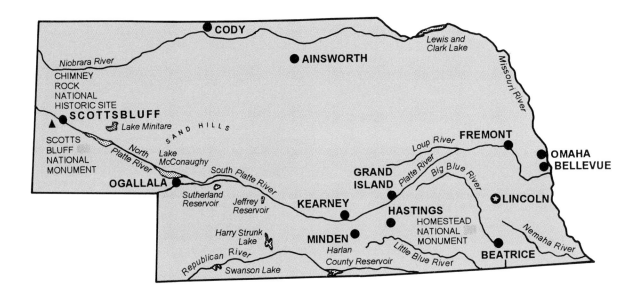

Land area:
> 77,355 square miles, of which 711 are inland water. Ranks 15th in size.

Major rivers:
> The Platte River system; the Missouri River, the Big Blue and Little Blue; the Loup; the Nemaha; the Niobrara; and the Republican.

Highest point: 5,426 ft. (Kimball County)

Major bodies of water:
> Harlan County Reservoir; Harry Strunk Lake; Jeffrey Reservoir; Johnson Lake; Lake McConaughy; Lake Minitare; Lewis and Clark Lake; Swanson Lake; and Sutherland Reservoir.

Climate:
> Average January temperature: 20.2° F
> Average July temperature: 77.7° F

Population: 1,605,603 (1992)
Rank: 36th
    1900: 1,066,300
    1854: 2,732 (territory)

Population of major cities (1992):

Omaha	335,719
Lincoln	191,972
Grand Island	39,487
Bellevue	30,982
Kearney	24,396
Fremont	23,680
Hastings	22,837

Ethnic breakdown by percentage (1990):

White	92.5%
African American	3.6%
Hispanic	2.3%
Asian/Pacific Islander	0.7%
Native American	0.7%
Other	0.1%

Economy:
    Mainly agricultural (wheat, corn, sorghum, soybeans, cattle, hogs, and poultry); manufacturing (food processing, machinery, and electronic equipment); and transportation.

State government:
    Legislature: Nebraska has the only unicameral (one-house) state legislature. Its 49 members are elected to serve 4-year terms.
    Governor: The governor, elected for a 4-year term, heads the executive branch of the state government.
    Courts: The state's highest court is the supreme court, which consists of a chief justice and 6 associate justices. Judges are appointed by the governor but must run for approval after serving 3 years.
State capital: Lincoln

State Flag

Nebraska's state flag features the gold-and-silver state seal on a blue background. The state legislature adopted this "state banner," as it was first called, in 1925. It officially became the state flag in 1963.

State Seal

The "Great Seal of the State of Nebraska," adopted in 1867, bears the date of statehood and the state motto. Its symbols include a blacksmith, sheaves of grain, a steamboat, a cabin, and a railroad train.

State Motto

"Equality before the law" is Nebraska's state motto.

State Nickname

Nebraska was called the "Treeplanter's State" from 1895 until World War II, when it became the "Cornhusker State" to honor the University of Nebraska's football team.

Places

Agate Fossil Beds National Monument, Harrison

Ak-Sar-Ben Aquarium, Gretna

Arbor Lodge State Park, Nebraska City

Boys Town, Omaha

Buffalo Bill Ranch State Historical Park, North Platte

Chimney Rock National Historic Site, Bayard

DeSoto National Wildlife Refuge, Blair

Ferguson House, Lincoln

Folsom Children's Zoo, Lincoln

Fort Atkinson State Historical Park, Omaha

Fort Hartstuff State Historical Park, Illyria

Fort Kearny State Historical Park, Kearney

Fort Niobrara National Wildlife Refuge, Valentine

Fort Robinson, Crawford

General Crook House, Omaha

George W. Norris Home, McCook

Great Plains Black History Museum, Omaha

Henry Doorly Zoo, Omaha

Homestead National Monument, Beatrice

Indian Cave State Park, Shubert

Lied Imax Theater, Hastings

Joslyn Art Museum, Omaha

to See

Mormon Pioneer Cemetery, Omaha

Museum of the Fur Trade, Chadron

Nebraska State Historical Society Museum, Lincoln

Neligh Mills, Neligh

Oglala National Grasslands, Crawford

Old Market, Omaha

Omaha Children's Museum, Omaha

Pike-Pawnee National Landmark, Guide Rock

Pioneer Village, Minden

Pony Express Station Restoration, Gothenburg

Ralph Mueller Planetarium, Lincoln

Roubidoux Pass, Bridgeport

Scotts Bluff National Monument, Scottsbluff

Sheldon Gallery of Art, University of Nebraska, Lincoln

Snake River Falls, Valentine

State Capitol Building, Lincoln

Strategic Air Command Museum, Bellevue

Stuhr Museum, Grand Island

Union Pacific Historical Museum, Omaha

Willa Cather Historical Center, Red Cloud

William Jennings Bryan Home, Lincoln

State Flower

Nebraska's state flower is the goldenrod. A perennial found throughout the United States, the goldenrod has hundreds of tiny yellow-gold flowers on each of its stalks.

State Bird

The western meadowlark, Nebraska's state bird, helps farmers by feeding on insects that damage crops.

State Tree

Nebraska's state tree is the cottonwood. One of the few tree species to grow naturally on the Great Plains, cottonwoods are most often found along rivers and streams.

Nebraska History

1682 Mississippi Valley region claimed for France

1720 Spanish expedition led by Pedro de Villasur defeated by Pawnees

1739 Mallet brothers explore the Platte River Valley

1803 U.S. acquires Nebraska through the Louisiana Purchase

1804 Lewis and Clark travel through Nebraska on their way to the Pacific Ocean

1819 Fort Atkinson constructed on Council Bluff

1819–20 Major Stephen Long maps South Platte area

1820 Slavery outlawed in Nebraska region

1823 First permanent settlement, in Bellevue

1832 First wagon train follows the Platte River Valley route westward

1838 Pierre Jean de Smet begins work among Nebraska's Indians

1840s Westward migration begins on the Oregon Trail

1854 Nebraska formally organized as a territory

1862 Homestead Act becomes law; first Nebraska homesteads claimed in 1863

1865 Union Pacific Railroad begins laying track westward from Omaha

1867 Nebraska admitted to Union

American

1492 Christopher Columbus reaches the New World

1607 Jamestown (Virginia) founded by English colonists

1620 *Mayflower* arrives at Plymouth (Massachusetts)

1754–63 French and Indian War

1765 Parliament passes Stamp Act

1775–83 Revolutionary War

1776 Signing of the Declaration of Independence

1788–90 First congressional elections

1791 Bill of Rights added to U.S. Constitution

1803 Louisiana Purchase

1812–14 War of 1812

1820 Missouri Compromise

1836 Battle of the Alamo, Texas

1846–48 Mexican-American War

1849 California Gold Rush

1860 South Carolina secedes from Union

1861–65 Civil War

1862 Lincoln signs Homestead Act

1863 Emancipation Proclamation

1865 President Lincoln assassinated (April 14)

1865–77 Reconstruction in the South

1866 Civil Rights bill passed

1881 President James Garfield shot (July 2)

History

1896 First Ford automobile is made

1898–99 Spanish-American War

1901 President William McKinley is shot (Sept. 6)

1917 U.S. enters World War I

1922 Nineteenth Amendment passed, giving women the vote

1929 U.S. stock market crash; Great Depression begins

1933 Franklin D. Roosevelt becomes president; begins New Deal

1941 Japanese attack Pearl Harbor (Dec. 7); U.S. enters World War II

1945 U.S. drops atomic bomb on Hiroshima and Nagasaki; Japan surrenders, ending World War II

1963 President Kennedy assassinated (November 22)

1964 Civil Rights Act passed

1965–73 Vietnam War

1968 Martin Luther King, Jr., shot in Memphis (April 4)

1974 President Richard Nixon resigns because of Watergate scandal

1979–81 Hostage crisis in Iran: 52 Americans held captive for 444 days

1989 End of U.S.-Soviet cold war

1991 Gulf War

1993 U.S. signs North American Free Trade Agreement with Canada and Mexico

Nebraska History

1874–77 Grasshoppers devastate crops on the state's farms

1877 Sioux leader Crazy Horse surrenders to the U.S. Army at Fort Robinson

1885 Arbor Day declared a legal holiday in Nebraska

1896 William Jennings Bryan is nominated for president by Democratic and Populist parties (Bryan also runs in 1900 and 1908)

1917 Father Flanagan opens Boys Town in Omaha

1932 State capitol building dedicated at Lincoln

1933 State government halts mortgage foreclosures during Great Depression

1934 Nebraska adopts a one-house state legislature

1939 Oil discovered at Falls City

1946 Omaha chosen as headquarters of Strategic Air Command (SAC)

1974 Gerald R. Ford becomes president after the resignation of Richard Nixon; first Nebraska-born president.

1982 Nebraska forbids sale of farms to out-of-state corporations

1986 Kay Orr elected governor

1992 Nebraska senator Bob Kerrey, a former governor, runs for the Democratic presidential nomination

Red Cloud (1822–1909)
Born in what is now part of Nebraska, the Oglala Sioux leader Red Cloud was one of the few Native American leaders to win a war against the U.S. Army.

J. Sterling Morton (1832–1902) The "Father of Arbor Day," Morton settled in the Nebraska Territory in 1854. Morton also served as U.S. secretary of agriculture (1893–97).

Michael Cudahy (1841–1910) Founder of the Cudahy Packing Company, this Irish-born businessman helped make Omaha one of America's major meatpacking centers.

William F. Cody (1846–1947) Known as

Buffalo Bill

"Buffalo Bill," this legendary army scout, frontiersman, and showman built a ranch at North Platte in 1878.

Susette La Flesche (1854–1903) The daughter of an Omaha tribe leader, Susette La Flesche campaigned for fair treatment of Native Americans.

Francis La Flesche (1857–1932) The brother of Susette La Flesche, Francis La Flesche also worked for Native American rights. He was a noted scholar and writer on Native American culture.

William Jennings Bryan (1860–1925) Born in Illinois, Bryan moved to Nebraska in 1887, where he edited an Omaha newspaper and practiced law. A three-time Democratic presidential candidate, Bryan also served as secretary of state (1913–15).

John J. Pershing (1860–1948) Commander of U.S. forces during World War I, Pershing spent part of his early career at the University of Nebraska, where he taught, earned a law degree, and organized the Pershing Rifles, a crack ROTC drill team.

George W. Norris (1861–1944) Norris represented Nebraska in both the House and the Senate from 1913 to 1943. A Republican, Norris was responsible for much important legislation in his long and distinguished career.

Roscoe Pound (1870–1964) Born in Lincoln, Pound was one of the most important and influential legal scholars of the 20th century.

Louise Pound (1872–1958) The sister of Roscoe Pound, Louise Pound was a noted writer and collector of folk tales. She taught at the University of Nebraska for more than half a century.

John G. Neihardt (1881–1973) Named Poet Laureate of Nebraska in 1922, Neihardt also wrote important works on Native American subjects, including *Black Elk Speaks* (1932).

Willa Cather (1873–1947) Born in Virginia but raised on the Nebraska plains, Cather, the state's best-known writer, published several novels with Nebraska themes, including *O Pioneers!* (1913), *My Antonia*

(1918), and *One of Ours* (1922), which won the Pulitzer Prize.

Edward J. Flanagan (1886–1948) This Irish-born Roman Catholic priest founded Boys Town, a home for troubled and neglected boys, in 1917.

Fred Astaire (1899–1987) Born Frederick Austerlitz in Omaha, this great dancer and choreographer starred in many stage and screen musicals.

Mari Sandoz (1901–66) Sandoz, a writer of both history and fiction, explored Western themes in many of her books, including a noted biography of the Sioux leader Crazy Horse.

Darryl F. Zanuck (1902–79) A native of Wahoo, this screenwriter and movie studio executive produced such classic films as *The Grapes of Wrath* (1940) and co-founded Twentieth Century Pictures, later Twentieth-Century Fox.

Henry Fonda (1905–82) Born in Grand Island, Fonda appeared in eighty-seven films and won two Academy Awards in an acting career that spanned more than forty years.

Loren Eiseley (1907–77) This Lincoln-born writer and educator explored the relationship between science and human behavior in such books as *Darwin's Century* (1958) and *The Firmament of Time* (1960).

Wright Morris (b. 1910) A novelist and photographer, Morris won the National Book Award for *Field of Vision* (1956).

Gerald R. Ford (b. 1913) Born in Omaha and originally named Leslie King, Ford served in the House of Representatives until 1973, when he was appointed vice president. He became the first Nebraskan in the White House when President Richard Nixon resigned in 1974, but lost to Jimmy Carter in the 1976 presidential race.

Marlon Brando (b. 1924) This controversial actor achieved his first success in the play *A Streetcar Named Desire* (1947). Among Brando's films are *On the Waterfront* (1954) and *The Godfather* (1972).

Malcolm X (1925–65) Born Malcolm Little in Omaha, he changed his name after becoming a member of the Nation of

Malcolm X

Islam. One of the most influential black leaders of the 1950s and 1960s, Malcolm X was assassinated in 1965.

Johnny Carson (b. 1925) The "King of Late Night TV" was born in Corning and began his career at Station WOW in Omaha. From 1962 to 1992 he was the host of NBC's "Tonight Show."

Robert Kerrey (b. 1943) Kerrey won the Congressional Medal of Honor in Vietnam before entering politics. He served as Nebraska's governor from 1983 to 1987 and was elected to the Senate in 1988. He unsuccessfully sought the Democratic presidential nomination in 1992.

Pictures in this volume:

Dover: 17, 34 (bottom), 38 (top)

Joslyn Art Museum: 8-9

Library of Congress: 7, 15, 16, 11, 13, 21, 23, 25 (bottom), 27, 29 (both), 44, 45, 46, 47, 50, 60, 61

Museum of New Mexico, Palace of the Governors: 12

National Archives: 30, 48-49

National Park Service: 18-19

Nebraska Department of Economic Development: 2, 51

Nebraska State Historical Society: 22, 25 (top), 26, 33, 34 (top), 36, 37, 39, 40, 41, 42, 43

Senator Kerrey's Office: 53 (bottom)

Smithsonian Institute: 31

University of Nebraska: 53 (top)

About the author:

Charles A. Wills is a writer, editor, and consultant specializing in American history. He has written, edited, or contributed to more than thirty books, including many volumes in The Millbrook Press's *American Albums from the Collections of the Library of Congress* series, as well as several titles in the *State Historical Albums* series. Wills lives in Dutchess County, New York.

Suggested reading:

Brown, Dee. *Wondrous Times on the Frontier*. New York: Harper Perennial, 1992.

Carpenter, Allan. *The New Enchantment of America: Nebraska*. Chicago: Childrens Press, 1978.

Cather, Willa. *My Antonia*. New York: Penguin Books, 1994.

—. *O Pioneers!* Thorndike, ME: Thorndike Press, 1986.

Creigh, Dorothy Weyer. *Nebraska: A Bicentennial History*. New York: Norton, 1977.

Hargrove, Jim. *America the Beautiful: Nebraska*. Chicago: Childrens Press, 1989.

Nicoll, Bruce. *Nebraska: A Pictorial History*. Lincoln: University of Nebraska Press, 1975.

Sandoz, Mari. *The Cattlemen*. Lincoln: University of Nebraska Press, 1978.

—. *Old Jules*. Lincoln: University of Nebraska Press, 1978.

Thompson, Kathleen. *Nebraska*. Milwaukee, WI: Raintree Publishers, 1988.

For more information contact:

Nebraska Division of Travel & Tourism
700 South 16th Street
P.O. Box 94666
Lincoln, NE 68509-4666
Tel: (800) 228-4307

Nebraska State Historical Society
1500 R Street, Box 82554
Lincoln, NE 68501
Tel: (402) 471-3270

Page numbers in *italics* indicate illustrations